WEEKLY WR READER®

EARLY LEARNING LIBRARY

LET'S READ ABOUT

Animals

CONOZCAMOS A LOS

animales

Dolphins/ Delfines

by/por Kathleen Pohl

Reading consultant/Consultora de lectura:
Susan Nations, M.Ed.,
author, literacy coach, consultant in literacy
development/autora, tutora de alfabetización,
consultora de desarrollo de la lectura

Please visit our web site at: www.garethstevens.com
For a free color catalog describing Weekly Reader® Early Learning Library's list
of high-quality books, call 1-877-445-5824 (USA) or 1-800-387-3178 (Canada).
Weekly Reader® Early Learning Library's fax: (414) 336-0164.

Library of Congress Cataloging-in-Publication Data

Pohl, Kathleen.
  [Dolphins. Spanish and English]
  Dolphins = Delfines / by/por Kathleen Pohl.
    p. cm. — (Let's read about animals = Conozcamos a los animales)
  Includes bibliographical references and index.
  ISBN-13: 978-0-8368-8005-2 (lib. bdg.)
  ISBN-13: 978-0-8368-8012-0 (softcover)
  1. Dolphins—Juvenile literature. I. Title. II. Title: Delfines.
  QL737.C432P6418   2007
  599.53—dc22   2006037319

This edition first published in 2007 by
Weekly Reader® Early Learning Library
A Member of the WRC Media Family of Companies
330 West Olive Street, Suite 100
Milwaukee, WI 53212 USA

Editor: Dorothy L. Gibbs
Art Direction: Tammy West
Cover design and page layout: Kami Strunsee
Picture research: Diane Laska-Swanke
Spanish translation: Tatiana Acosta and Guillermo Gutiérrez

Picture credits: Cover, title, pp. 7, 13, 17 © Doug Perrine/Auscape; p. 5 © Steven David Miller/Auscape;
pp. 8-9 Kami Strunsee/© Weekly Reader® Early Learning Library; p. 11 © Tom Walmsley/naturepl.com;
p. 15 © Todd Pusser/naturepl.com; p. 19 © Becca Saunders/Auscape; p. 21 © François Gohier/Auscape

Printed in the United States of America

1 2 3 4 5 6 7 8 9 10 10 09 08 07 06

Note to Educators and Parents

Reading is such an exciting adventure for young children! They are beginning to integrate their oral language skills with written language. To encourage children along the path to early literacy, books must be colorful, engaging, and interesting; they should invite the young reader to explore both the print and the pictures.

The *Let's Read About Animals* series is designed to help children read and learn about the special characteristics and behaviors of the intriguing featured animals. Each book is an informative nonfiction companion to one of the colorful and charming fiction books in the *Animal Storybooks* series.

Each book in the *Let's Read About Animals* series is specially designed to support the young reader in the reading process. The familiar topics are appealing to young children and invite them to read — and reread — again and again. The full-color photographs and enhanced text further support the student during the reading process.

In addition to serving as wonderful picture books in schools, libraries, homes, and other places where children learn to love reading, these books are specifically intended to be read within an instructional guided reading group. This small group setting allows beginning readers to work with a fluent adult model as they make meaning from the text. After children develop fluency with the text and content, the books can be read independently. Children and adults alike will find these books supportive, engaging, and fun!

— Susan Nations, M.Ed., author/literacy coach/
consultant in literacy development

Nota para los maestros y los padres

¡Leer es una aventura tan emocionante para los niños pequeños! A esta edad están comenzando a integrar su manejo del lenguaje oral con el lenguaje escrito. Para animar a los niños en el camino de la lectura incipiente, los libros deben ser coloridos, estimulantes e interesantes; deben invitar a los jóvenes lectores a explorar la letra impresa y las ilustraciones.

Conozcamos a los animales es una nueva colección diseñada para que los niños conozcan las características y comportamientos de los interesantes animales que se presentan. Cada libro es un texto informativo de no ficción que acompaña a uno de los libros de ficción en lengua inglesa de la colección *Animal Storybooks*.

Cada libro de la serie *Conozcamos a los animales* está especialmente diseñado para ayudar a los jóvenes lectores en el proceso de lectura. Los temas familiares llaman la atención de los niños y los invitan a leer una y otra vez. Las fotografías a todo color y el tamaño de la letra ayudan aún más al estudiante en el proceso de lectura.

Además de servir como maravillosos libros ilustrados en escuelas, bibliotecas, hogares y otros lugares donde los niños aprenden a amar la lectura, estos libros han sido especialmente concebidos para ser leídos en un grupo de lectura guiada. Este contexto permite que los lectores incipientes trabajen con un adulto que domina la lectura mientras van determinando el significado del texto. Una vez que los niños dominan el texto y el contenido, el libro puede ser leído de manera independiente. ¡Estos libros les resultarán útiles, estimulantes y divertidos a niños y a adultos por igual!

— Susan Nations, M.Ed., autora/tutora de alfabetización/
consultora de desarrollo de la lectura

Have you seen **dolphins** at a zoo or a sea park? They are fun to watch!

¿Alguna vez has visto **delfines** en un zoológico o parque marino? ¡Son muy divertidos!

This dolphin is the kind most people see. It is a **bottlenose dolphin**. Can you guess how it got its name?

Éste es el tipo de delfín que más gente conoce. Es un **delfín mular**, también llamado "nariz de botella". ¿Adivinas por qué le pusieron este otro nombre?

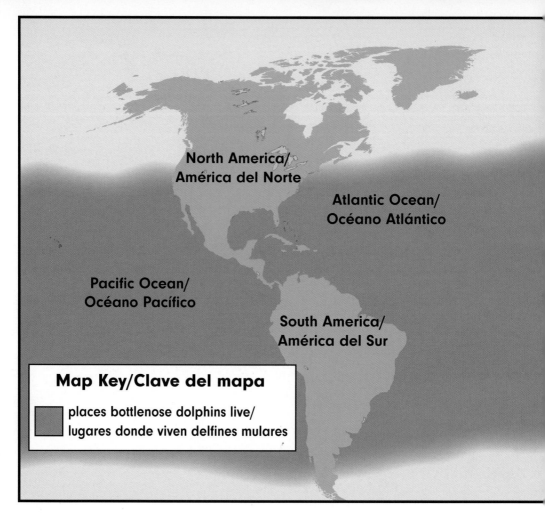

North America/
América del Norte

Atlantic Ocean/
Océano Atlántico

Pacific Ocean/
Océano Pacífico

South America/
América del Sur

Map Key/Clave del mapa

places bottlenose dolphins live/
lugares donde viven delfines mulares

Dolphins live in oceans and seas all over the world.

Los delfines viven en mares y océanos de todo el mundo.

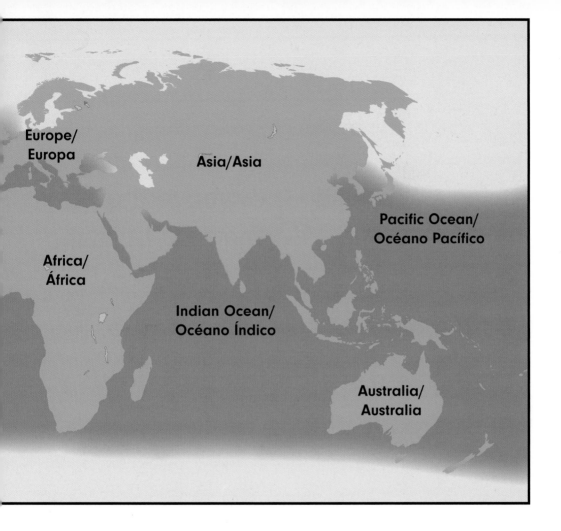

The map shows where most bottlenose dolphins live.

El mapa muestra dónde viven la mayoría de los delfines mulares.

Dolphins swim fast! They move their **flippers** and **flukes**, or tail fins, to swim.

¡Los delfines nadan muy rápido! Para nadar, mueven sus **aletas anteriores** y sus **aletas caudales**, o de la cola.

**flippers/
aletas anteriores**

**flukes/
aletas caudales**

Dolphins swim together to stay safe.
A group of dolphins is called a **pod**.

Para protegerse, los delfines nadan
en grupo. Un grupo de delfines se
llama **manada**.

A dolphin cannot breathe underwater. It swims to the surface for air. It breathes through a **blowhole** on top of its head.

Un delfín no puede respirar debajo del agua. Para buscar aire, sale a la superficie. Respira a través de un **espiráculo**, un agujero en la parte superior de la cabeza.

blowhole/
espiráculo

Dolphins eat fish. They herd fish into big groups to catch them. Dolphins hunt together to help each other.

Los delfines se alimentan de peces. Para atraparlos, los acorralan hasta formar grupos grandes. Los delfines cazan juntos para ayudarse.

An **auntie** is a special kind of helper in a pod. She helps a mother dolphin take care of her **calf**.

En la manada, una **tía** se encarga de ayudar a una madre delfín en el cuidado de la **cría**.

calf/
cría

Dolphins love to leap, splash, and dive. They always look like they are having fun. And they are always smiling!

A los delfines les encanta saltar, chapotear y zambullirse. Parece que siempre se están divirtiendo. ¡Y no paran de sonreír!

Glossary/Glosario

blowhole — the hole on a dolphin's head through which it takes in air and spouts water to breathe

calf — a young dolphin

flippers — armlike body parts that move back and forth to help dolphins and other sea animals swim

flukes — the flat fins at the end of a dolphin's tail

herd — to force animals into a close group by chasing them or surrounding them

surface — the top or highest level of a body of water

---

acorralar — perseguir o rodear animales para obligarlos a agruparse

aletas anteriores — partes del cuerpo similares a brazos que un delfín u otro animal marino mueve para nadar

aletas caudales — aletas planas al final de la cola de un delfín

cría — delfín joven

espiráculo — agujero en la cabeza por el que un delfín toma aire y arroja agua al respirar

superficie — la parte superior de una masa de agua

For More Information/Más información

Books

The Dolphin Family. Animal Families (series). Bev Harvey (Chelsea Clubhouse)

Dolphins: Fins, Flippers, and Flukes. Adele D. Richardson (Bridgestone Books)

Little Dolphin's Big Leap. Animal Storybooks (series). Rebecca Johnson (Gareth Stevens)

Libros

Los delfines. Animales marinos salvajes (series). Melissa and Brandon Cole (Blackbirch Press)

Los delfines. Los animales (series). Donna Bailey (Steck-Vaughn)

Delfines. Mamífero marino (series). Sarah Palmer (Rourke Publishing)

Index/Índice

blowholes 14, 15
bottlenose dolphins 6, 8, 9
breathing 14
calves 18, 19
flippers 10, 11
flukes 10, 11
hunting 16
leaping 20
pods 12, 18
swimming 10, 12, 14

aletas anteriores 10, 11
aletas caudales 10, 11
cazar 16
crías 18, 19
delfines mulares 6, 8, 9
espiráculos 14, 15
manadas 12, 18
nadar 10, 12, 14
respirar 14
saltar 20

About the Author/Información sobre la autora

Kathleen Pohl has written and edited many children's books. Among them are animal tales, rhyming books, retold classics, and the forty-book series *Nature Close-Ups*. She and her husband, Bruce, live in the middle of beautiful Wisconsin woods and share their home with six goats, a llama, and all kinds of wonderful woodland creatures.

Kathleen Pohl ha escrito y corregido muchos libros infantiles. Entre ellos hay cuentos de animales, libros de rimas, versiones nuevas de cuentos clásicos y la serie de cuarenta libros *Nature Close-Ups*. Kathleen vive con su marido, Bruce, en medio de los bellos bosques de Wisconsin. Ambos comparten su hogar con seis cabras, una llama y todo tipo de maravillosos animales del bosque.